PRAYERS
that
GOD
will
HEAR

And Short Stories

MARY A. LASER

Archway Publishing books may be ordered through booksellers or by contacting:

Archway Publishing
1663 Liberty Drive
Bloomington, IN 47403
www.archwaypublishing.com
1 (888) 242-5904

ISBN: 978-1-4808-8951-4 (sc)
ISBN: 978-1-4808-8952-1 (e)

Library of Congress Control Number: 2020905602

Print information available on the last page.

Archway Publishing rev. date: 03/13/2020

The bible says, "You reap what you sow"
Galatians 6:7

Acknowledgements

I wish to thank the following people who assisted me in preparing my book to be published. I thank each and every one of you in alphabetical order:

Cindy Sappe Dreyer

Christopher J Sappe (cover designer)

Jean E. Wolff (assisted in preparation for publishing)

My relatives who contributed interesting stories:

Kaitlin Hrozencik, my grand niece and
god child (great fiction stories)

Joseph Venditto Jr., my grand nephew (his
extremely interesting fiction story)

Thank you one and all and God bless you.

Contents

Prayers That God Will Hear

Our lord Jehovah is his name. He is responsible for creating heaven and earth.

Many people do not understand that we do have a wonderful lord who made the universe and everything in it that walks, lies and lives in the ocean. We can see all these things and even catch some to eat. Since we see all these things and know they exist, we believe they exist.

We cannot see our lord, but those who know and understand him know that he is there.

When Jesus was on this earth and knew that he would be killed so our sins could be forgiven. He told peter he had to go away and he should pray to the father through him so that his prayers will be heard.

(New world translation of the Holy Scripture--------all versions)

This is the correct way to pray. Many people pray to the Virgin Mary and other saints, but they cannot hear you, they are dead and sleeping until the resurrection.

If you want our lord Jehovah to hear you there are three things you must do.

1. All prayers must be directed to god Jehovah in the name of his son Jesus.
2. Whatever you pray for must be in accordance with the will of Jehovah.

3. When you pray, you must have complete faith that your prayer will be answered.

If there is any doubt, then it will not be answered.

Also, realize that your prayer may either be answered immediately or at some later time. God will determine the proper time to answer your prayer. It is up to him when to answer your prayer, not you. It is also up to him how he will answer your prayer. He knows better than you do as to what you need and how to provide it. But rest assured it will always be

To your benefit. Sometimes the answer will be "no" because you prayed for something that would not be in your best interest. In addition to praying for something to happen, you must do your best to bring it about. The old saying, "god helps those who help themselves," applies.

This book is being written to help people who do not know our lord Jehovah and his son Jesus. And for those who do not believe in them. When you read this book, it will help you understand and change your life.

I want you to know that I am recovering from a stroke and do not remember the exact place in the bible for references. So, it is mainly to teach you how to pray so god will hear you, and learn that he does answer you.

All of you who do not know about our god, Jehovah, this author would like to tell you many of the true things that have happened to her and how our lord, Jehovah, helped her. This first story shows that our lord hears and remembers even after death.

Where I want my ashes

My sister lived just fifty feet from her pier and water. We spent many wonderful visits with her. She taught our young relatives how to fish and crab, resulting in many delicious crab feasts. Each time, she would tell me that when she died, she wanted her ashes to be placed under her pier. Nineteen years later she could not handle the boat or water coming into the house, so we sold the property and bought one for her away from the water. A year after she moved away from the island, she passed away. My two nieces and one nephew took her ashes to her neighbor's pier. The water was smooth, clear, and very still that day. I was on the phone with my niece because I was unable to attend. She was giving me a word by word description of what was happening. The first thing she said was, "We are here and are ready to open the urn and spill the ashes into the water". There was absolute silence as my niece poured the ashes into the water

Then in a loud voice she yelled, "Oh my god, you will not believe this!" I asked "what is wrong?" She replied "nothing is wrong, the water started rippling as soon as the ashes went in, and now they are moving down to her pier! We are standing here with our mouths open!" I said, "Maybe it's a coincidence, see what happens when you put the flowers in the water." My niece replied, "the water is still now so we are going to put in the flowers." When they put the flowers in the water she screamed, "They are doing the same thing, they are going toward her pier."

When the flowers reached the pier the water stopped rippling and became absolutely calm again. I could hear them laughing and crying.

So the lord gave my loveable, stubborn sister her final wish after all.

My Life

I was born in the year of 1929. The stock market crashed, and people were committing suicide because they lost everything. Our mother died in pregnancy. Our dad had a job in the mines which paid very little money. We had no help from anyone. Starting at the age of eight, I had to find a job because our family of six boys and six girls were destitute! Fortunately, at my age I was tall and could pass for someone aged 15. I went to the restaurant on the corner. The owners living quarters were on top of the restaurant.

The woman and man who owned it interviewed me. They asked if I knew how to clean, wash and iron clothes, and scrub floors and bathrooms. I answered yes to all of those things, and they said, to make certain that you can-you must go upstairs and prove it. I thanked the lord with all of my heart that they did not ask my age. I went upstairs and did all they asked. Five hours later I came down and they went upstairs and inspected. They came down and said they were very happy with my work and told me I was hired and handed me my pay of $1.00 they told me to come back next Saturday and every Saturday after that! I was so happy to have that dollar. I ran as fast as I could home and gave it to my dad. He asked where I got it and I told him. He thanked me and told me to keep up the good work.

I worked there until I entered high school and then I was able to get a job in the sewing factory near our home. That was another blessing from our lord!

After graduating high school, I was offered a job as a baby caring nurse. They actually paid us! I had to leave Pennsylvania and move to New York. After one year, I graduated from the town hospital.

I then decided to enter the military for three years. I was able to send money home because I did not go out and spend my money

Like so many others did. I was assigned to an army hospital during my tour of duty and was invited to return as a civilian because

They liked my administrative abilities and needed someone in the army dental corps area. A time came when they were cutting back, so they could hire more veterans. Thank the lord I was a veteran and not fired. I remained there for 33 ½ years before I retired.

In the meantime, besides continuing my education at the military's expense, I took a job as a part-time realtor and began doing income tax and financial work, budgeting, etc. At which I became successful. Another blessing from our lord!

My family was in a better financial position. I met and married a very nice southern gentleman who was in college. I stopped my

Education and took an additional position to help him graduate sooner, and he did.

I met a sergeant major when I was in the military and the army assigned him to the same army hospital. He became very close friends with my husband and me. One day he asked me if I would go with him to train as a Realtor. Since my husband worked nights and went to school during the day, I agreed. I prayed about it and asked the lord if we would be successful, and if so, to please show me a sign of an angel. And he did! I was so excited that I began to pray more and more every night.

We became so successful, we sold more properties than the full-time realtors! Years before I retired, I began praying. When things got rough and I was diagnosed with my cancer. I prayed for help and our lord got me through it all three times.

One night several years later, I asked the lord if I would be successful if we bought houses, fixed them up, and rented them. I thought it would be good for when we retired. This was the first time I ever heard a voice!

The voice was soft, but I heard it say yes. I was so happy to hear that voice, I cried with joy. It was then that the three of us being very close, made a pact. If any one of us died, the remaining ones would take care of each other. And we did. My husband passed away and the now command sergeant major, true to his word, began caring for me. He took over, and ultimately, we married. Three days before my second husband passed away, I had a stroke which paralyzed me on my left side. I was told I had a week to live. My family prayed for me. The lord sent my dearest friend, who is a physician. She flew up and asked for more tests and for a new neurologist. Since she was my physician. The hospital accommodated her. The new neurologist read the test results and said to her, "In all my years I have never seen anything like this! The blood is receding, but this is a miracle! Look! Her cranium is like that of a new born baby. She is not going to die, but she will be in a nursing home for seven months or more." When my physician told me this, I put my hand on the top of my head and it was open just as he said.

It is currently closed, except for two finger-tip spaces that are still open. When I was discharged to a nursing home, I picked one that my friend's parents owned it stated

They gave physical therapy seven days a week. When I arrived, I found out they only did therapy five days a week. My brother called me and reminded me to ask the lord what to do. So I did. I had been meditating for 70 years, so I was at the point where I could hear his voice when I asked for something. My prayer: dear lord jehovah, if it is your will, would you please tell me what to do so I can get well soon, I need to show my nephew where all my things are located. I am asking in the name of your son jesus. The voice said........do it yourself.

My eyes opened and my right hand was open in front of my face. I said thank you and used my right hand to do therapy on my left hand. My left hand was working in three days. I did

Not let the nursing home know. I got my arm working next. Then I called the best aide who had helped me when my husband was in hospice at home, and needed round the clock care. He was able t0 stay after hours because I had a private room. I was able to be discharged in seven weeks for home therapy.

After therapy I was able to walk holding on. Physically I am in pretty good shape, but my mind is not back to normal. Sometimes I am

Actually lucid, and other times, I cannot remember how many years it has been since my stroke.

I then met my new husband. I looked like a 100-year-old mummy, but he didn't care. He had been a care giver for his wife for four years and promised that he would take care of me. We dated for two years and then

Married. When we first met, I had wrinkles and marks on my face. He had retired from the battlefield and had black marks and wrinkles over his face, and also terrible marks on his head. We both felt the same way.

It is not looks that count, but what's on the inside. I left my home and moved to another city into his home. One day I told him I would like to pray and see if the lord would give me some kind of cream to clean us up. He thought that was nice. That night I prayed and said the prayer: Lord Jehovah would you please give me something I could put in a cream form that will remove all the marks from our faces and my husband's head. I am asking in the name of your son, Jesus, and thank you in the name of your son, Jesus.

I heard a voice say, "hyaluronic acid and vitamin c." I felt so excited I forced myself to wake up and ordered the items. I mixed them together and called it the "true miracle cream." It worked, not quickly, but enough for my husband to say that I should get a patent on it. I said, "Okay, tomorrow I will send for the forms."

The next morning, we woke up and turned on the tv. Someone was saying, "ladies and gentlemen, I have the best thing for age marks and wrinkles: hyaluronic acid and vitamin c!" My husband said, "There goes your patent!" "Oh no," I said, "I will go back in and ask for another item so that I will not infringe on his patent." I immediately went into prayer and I received something I was not expecting. I heard a voice loud and clear, "You did not stay long enough!" Then came a list of many more items. So, I learned my lesson. Do not break out of prayer just because you get excited!

The items, minus the amounts needed were, hyaluronic acid, vitamin c, retinol, fruit stem cell, wrinkle cream, frankincense and myrrh, as well as medical marijuana cbd.

Do you not believe in miracles?

Read on

Miracle #1

In the year 2004, I felt a lump in my breast and went to the doctor who insisted that I should have a string biopsy. I did not want a string biopsy, but he made the appointment and my husband was to take me to the hospital the next day. That night I told the lord that I really did not want the string biopsy, and I would rather they take out the lump and then have it biopsied. Needless to say, I did not sleep very well that night. The next morning just as I was waking up, I heard this very light voice in my ear saying, "do not worry dear you will be ok." I thought I was not quite awake and still dreaming. I dressed and we went to the hospital. After six mammograms they could not find the lump, so they gave up and said it may have been a cyst that broke. As I was leaving the ward, this very elderly black nurse who was very sweet, came over to me and said, "do you know how blessed you are?" I answered, "Yes, I do, and I thank the lord for it every day." I went back to the oncologist and he found the lump again. He wanted a biopsy, but I told him no—take it out and then biopsy it, which he later did. This was the first miracle that the lord gave me.

Miracle 2

In 2007 my husband was very ill as having mini strokes more often each day. One day he and I went to lunch with our best friend. On our way out of the restaurant, he just went down! We could not pick him up and I prayed, "Dear lord, please send someone to help us!" Almost out of nowhere this young, strong man came over and asked if he could help. We were so thankful. He picked my husband up like a baby and put him in the car. By the time we reached home, he was feeling better. But I had already dialed 911 and told them to meet us there. He was sitting on the sofa when the paramedics came in and he did not want to go to the hospital saying he was fine. I asked the paramedics to check his mouth—he had had a stroke. They agreed and told my husband that he had to go to the hospital. He stated, "Well, I can certainly walk to the ambulance," which he did three days later, he had another stroke and was paralyzed from the neck down. I went to see him and there were tears in his eyes. I asked the lord to put the right words in my mouth to help him. I asked him if he was afraid, to blink once for yes and twice for no. He blinked once. Then, just as if I had rehearsed it, the following words came out, "do not worry sweetheart, they have this tube in your mouth and they have to make sure you do not move from your neck down, so it will not move and injure you." Immediately, his eyes brightened up and I knew he would be ok. I told him they would be taking it out on Sunday which would give all the family and friends time to come to see him and say their goodbyes. They were instructed not to tell him he was dying or that we were going to pull the plug. So many people came, and he was really happy and could understand everything they were reminiscing about. Come Saturday night, they told us he was beginning to slip away. That night I prayed to the lord saying, "Dear lord, I never asked you for a sign before, but would you please send me a sign so I can go on Sunday and have a bright and sunny disposition. Please send me a 'cricket', my husband liked crickets." I prayed and cried and prayed. Come Sunday morning, I was to meet with my niece as she was going to take me to the hospital. My husband and I were going to renew our wedding vows that day. When I woke up Sunday, I went into the kitchen and remembered I did not alert my sister-in-law that my husband was dying.my niece arrived and came into my home. When she reached the end of the counter, I looked up to say hi and when I did, her eyes were wide open and so was her mouth. She looked frightened! I asked her what was wrong. She replied, "There is a big bug on the floor next to your chair and we have to get rid of it- I hate bugs!" I said, "oh honey that is a cricket, a sign that god sent to me." She said. No he did not, get rid of it.

She had me so flustered that I forgot to tell her to take a picture. I asked her to give me one of the big red plastic cups. In the meantime, the cricket did not move. I gently put it over the cricket and the cricket still did not move. We slipped a piece of paper under the cup, and the cricket still did not move. My niece carried it to the backdoor and I watched through the window as she took away the cup. I heard the cricket sing as it jumped out up into the air and disappeared-in the air! I knew that the good lord had answered my prayer.

We were able to renew our vows and I was able to tell my husband the doctors would be removing the tube tonight without crying. The doctor told me I should go home and rest. I kissed my husband on the forehead and said, "Goodnight sweetheart. I will see you in the morning." He passed away comfortably and happy.

Here is the prayer for all to learn. It will help change your life for the better:

> "Lord Jehovah, if it is your will would you please, (and say what you want, be detailed), then say I am asking you in the name of your son Jesus. And I thank you in the name of your son Jesus." Sometimes the answer will take a while and sometimes it happens quickly.

Miracle #3

One day it was raining heavily and was supposed to continue most of the day. The home therapist was at my home and it was time for her to leave. I asked if she wanted to stay over until it subsided but she said no she wanted to go home. I taught her the prayer and we said it together. Our prayer went like this: "lord Jehovah if it is your will, would you please allow the rain to stop until my therapist can make it home on dry roads, she lives a long way from here, we are asking you in the name of your son Jesus". I walked her to the door and we stepped out on the porch, the rain stopped.

She called when she reached home. When she went into the house it started raining again.

She said her husband did not believe her. And she laughed and said "would you like to ask my patient?"

Miracle 4:

We were housecleaning and found many things we wanted to take to an antique dealer. It started raining while we were on the road. Our friend came with us to drive and help us move numerous boxes to the car. Because of the rain, I started my prayer: "lord Jehovah, if it is your will, would you stop the rain until we reach the building, deliver our boxes and return home. I am asking in the name of your son Jesus, and I thank you in the name of your son Jesus." The rain reduced to a drizzle and stopped when we reached the building, they sent two men to bring in the boxes from our vehicle. We then left to return home and there was no rain. After we were home, the rain started again and lasted most of the night.

You must regard the prayer to our lord as done and keep the faith, and you will be amazed how your life will change!

Miracle #5

My niece passed away and I am godmother to both of her children. I thank the lord every day that I was able to get my goddaughter through college. She graduated cum laud.

One day before graduation my goddaughter said to me, "I'm afraid I will not make an in psychology." I asked if she had studied hard on it, and she said yes. So, I told her that as long as you have studied hard, you will get you're a. I told her to repeat after me, and she said the prayer "Lord Jehovah, if it is your will, please allow me to make and A in psychology so that I can graduate cum laud. I am asking in the name of your son, Jesus, and thank you in the name of your son, Jesus." The next day the grades came out and she got an A! She immediately came to my house (she lives two blocks away) and literally danced with joy! She said "you were right! You were right!" "Thank you, Thank you!" I said "I will accept the thanks for teaching you the prayer, but remember it is our lord who answered it and his son who you need to thank!" She said "I will, every day in prayer."

Miracle #6

The auction house miracle:
When I met my current husband, I moved into his house. His house was much smaller than mine. So when I saw an auction house that was beautiful on the outside and large. I said to my husband, "look at this big, beautiful house! The area is really nice and it's close to the air force base where we receive our medical treatments. I would like to ask the lord if I could have it, what do you think?" He replied, "go ahead if you want to." I called the broker and will never forget him. I explained to him that I had never bought an auction house before, so I asked what was the first thing I had to do. He said, "go in early so if someone comes in more than you, you have a chance to change your bid." I said "okay, I will call you in the morning and let you know where

I want to be placed. I definitely am going to bid." The bidding was to start at 10:00 a.m., but I wanted to pray to see if it would be ok. My prayer was: "lord jehovah if it is your will please let me get this house, it has more room and is closer to the hospital. If you are willing, would you please not allow anyone to come in after my bid. I'm asking in the name of your son jesus and I thank you in the name of your son jesus." The voice said "go ahead."

The next morning I called the broker and told him to place my name at number 7, which means completion in heaven. "Oh no! You will lose it!" he replied. "No, the lord said I could have it." I told him. He said, "You are deluding yourself! I have been in this business for years and no one ever stopped at a bid at that number!" I explained, "The lord said it is mine. Do you know anything about the lord and the bible at all?" "No." He said. "Well, you will be a believer today. The auction starts in three minutes, put me in or leave me out!"

Not wanting to lose a potential sale, he put me in at number 7. Bidding started with low bid numbers one to number ten. Then my bid number, 1,2,3,4,5,6,7. No bids! Winner! Number 7!! My broker screamed into the phone, "How did you do that, can you teach me how?" I told him I would be happy to teach him how to pray. But he never called to learn.

My husband had a longtime friend who was a locksmith. We had dinner with him every Thursday. When he came, my husband and he were talking and he said, "Your wife really has guts! We could open that door and find flooding, mold, etc." I replied, "I do not want to hear one negative word come out of your mouth."

I was not permitted to see the inside of the house until after the settlement. Then I found out that they did not have a key for the house, so they gave me $700 to hire a Locksmith. My husband's friend opened it for $100. I could not walk very well at that time, so I stayed in the car and five minutes later the garage door opened, and my husband and

His friend came out with big smiles and said "this is a beautiful house." I said, "Did you think the lord would give me a bad house!"

Now here is where I learned a lesson. They both helped me into the house. It was lovely, but it did not have a bedroom on the first floor and the steps were too steep. There was not enough room for me to use my electric chair. I forgot to ask for a bedroom on the first floor!! They both told me to just put it on the market and resell it. I said, "I cannot do that! My policy is that I do not sell or rent a house that I would not want to live in. I will update it and then put it on the market." So, I did. After it was completed my broker called me and asked me to let him sell the house. I knew he could not sell it, but I agreed. My broker and his manager came to the house to sign the selling paperwork. "I will give you three weeks." I told them. "Oh no!" They replied. "We require 90 days." I asked them who owned the house, and they said that I did. "Then you take three weeks, or you do not get the opportunity to try to sell it."

Long story: he was supposed to call me, but I had to call him. When I asked if he had a contract for me, he said, "no, but a lot of people are looking at it and they say it is beautiful." I told him, "I did not give you the house to show, I gave it to you to sell. Did you say the prayer? He said, "no, I thought you did." I told him, when it was in my hands and I was responsible for it, I did. When it

Was in your hands it was your responsibility. Obviously, you did not understand that! Your time is up tomorrow, so make sure you take your sign down."

I looked for and found another realtor. We said the prayer, and the house sold in three days for more than the asking price and enough to cover the rest of the college tuition for my goddaughter. Please remember, to be really detailed when you ask for something. And, as you can see, the prayer can be used in many different ways and for many types of things.

Biblical examples of dream interpretation

Joseph's dreams of authority over his family (genesis 37:5-11)
The dreams of the cupbearer and the baker (genesis 40)
Pharaoh's dreams of feast and famine (genesis 41:1-36)
The midianite's dream of defeat (judges 7:13-14)
Nebuchadnezzar's dream of the statue (daniel 2)
Nebuchadnezzar's dream of the fallen tree (daniel 4)
Daniel's dream of the four beasts (daniel 7:1-8)

There are other examples of visions and dreams in the bible, as god did reveal his plans in dreams to certain individuals.

An unexpected helping hand

By
Mary a. Laser

I sat in the office of the doctor, next to a very nice-looking woman with dark brown hair and eyes. Her facial skin was clear and smooth, and she appeared to be in her middle thirties. Her reason for the doctor was that she was very depressed and could not figure out why. Her husband got up from the chair next to her and walked off. She turned her head toward me and said, "I believe he is the reason for all of this." I felt sorry for her and she could sense it because she said, "do you mind if I ask you a question?" "Of course not" I said. "Are you married? And, if so, are you happy?" I smiled and said, "I was married, I was happy then, but my husband had died." She saw her husband returning and asked if she could talk with me later. I told her yes, I was early for my appointment and figured I would read an interesting book I had not finished. She was called into her appointment and her husband said he would meet her at home and left. Ten minutes later she returned and said she was glad her husband left so she could talk with me. After telling me about her youth and younger days up to the time she met her husband, she was very happy.

She continued telling me that they had agreed to save as much money as they could from both of their positions for a home. Soon the nurse said it was my turn, so I quickly wrote my name, address and telephone number on the note pad I carried in my purse. That evening she called and came over and continued from where she left off at the doctor's office we became good friends and did many things together. She no longer complained of being depressed. If there was a time when she was extremely sad, she stayed at my home for the night and the next day she was fine and went to work. She continued, explaining "and save we did. We had quite a substantial amount saved so we could put a large down payment on a house we both loved. We set a time with the salesman to sign the contract.

Two days before we were to do this, he told me he needed a lot of money for his mother, so we had to wait for the house. I was shocked and disappointed but I had no choice to say no because he had already taken the money out of our account.

Time went on and he again needed more money, which he removed from the account. That was the beginning of my depression. I continued to work hard and saved all I could. One day I received a telephone call from his mother. She was living overseas in Germany, so we rarely talked with her.

His father was deceased, and he had no siblings. He was not home at the time, so I asked how she was feeling. She told me she felt fine. I told her that her son had said that she needed a substantial amount of money and that he removed it from our bank account for her." She replied, "That was not true, I do not need any money. What did he do with it?" I was shocked and said, "I do not know, but he should be home soon, and he better have a good explanation."

He was late coming home that night and I told him his mother called and said she did not need any money. His face turned red and he screamed at me asking why I was checking on him. We did not communicate for months, and I stopped putting money into our joint account. I opened one for myself and was determined not to give a cent of it to him. He had already emptied our joint account so I closed the account. Just before Christmas he asked me for a divorce. I said, "no, that is against the law of our lord Jehovah." He laughed and said, "I am going to do it anyway." I replied, "why not just separate for a year and see what happens. If you still want it, I will agree. I will put it in writing and give you half of my savings." When he heard that, he agreed. I asked him if he would tell me if he was cheating on me. He said, "Yes, from the day of our wedding." "Then why did you marry me?" I asked. He laughed and said, "Because her divorce was not final, but it is now, and we want to marry." I told him, "well, you can wait another year and if you still want a divorce, I will give it to you." We saw an attorney and signed the paperwork. He immediately packed some of his clothing and told me he would return for the remainder at another time but would call first. The year was almost ending and the day before Christmas, he called and asked if he could visit. I was so happy to hear from him, I said, "yes, come at five o'clock for dinner today." Both I and the table were ready.

The doorbell rang, and I was at the door waiting and immediately opened it. I was shocked to see that he looked like he was ill. He came in and I gave him a hug. He burst into tears and said, "I want to come home." I, then burst into tears of joy and said, "Yes, yes!" He told me his lover was a terrible person and that was why her husband divorced her. He went on to explain, "She spent most of her salary on items for herself. She did not cook, so we had to eat out for all our dinner meals. When I had the flu, she would not take care of me, saying she did not want to catch it. She spent all of her days shopping. I just could not take it anymore!" That is when I

Remembered we had a separation and not a divorce. I prayed to our lord Jehovah and Jesus, asking them for him to take me back. I learned my lesson well. We both had dinner and I gave him a good chest and back rub and helped him into bed.

On Christmas morning he came to the breakfast table and said he felt fine. We hugged each other and exclaimed that this was the most wonderful gift from each other we could have received—together again! They are now celebrating their tenth anniversary and called me to celebrate with them saying, "We want you to share this great day with us. It would not have been possible without you! We both give our heartfelt thanks to you and ask our lord to have many, many more years with you."

Love at first picture

Fiction
By
Mary a. Laser

Gp's wife was deceased four years. He made no attempt to try to find someone. One day his daughter told him that he should go on the internet and try to find someone who would be a good companion or a more serious relationship. He searched for women in his area and found none that appealed to him. Finally, he said to himself, "one more try and then that is it." So, he began searching the profiles once again and found a picture of a woman who really touched him. He found that she was 400 miles away and looking for someone in the 100-mile range. He said, "I think I love this picture, so I am going to write to her anyway." He did, and he received a response that said, "I really like your profile, but you must know that I am older than you are, but not too much, and you are so far away." He responded and told her that age is only a number and planes can fly the distance. Annie's husband was deceased for almost a year after two long years of illness. Her niece told her it was time to look for someone else. She encouraged her to go on the internet and set up an account.

After going through viewing 124 male profiles, she was ready to give up. "One more time and then I will quit", she said to herself. Then she received an e-mail from gp. She checked his picture and profile and said to herself, "I could really love this guy", and so she responded to his e-mail. After returning an e-mail to gp, she did not receive a response back, so she thought that he probably found someone closer to his area. But this was not true, she had accidently blocked him from contacting her. He could not understand why she was still sending him mail, but he could not send an answer. Being a clever fellow, he contacted the dating site and asked them to contact her to be sure that she did indeed want him blocked from writing to her. When she received the e-mail from the dating site, she replied that she did not block him intentionally and would they unblock him for her. They sent her an e-mail telling her how to unblock him, which she immediately did. Since she only had three days left on the site, she sent her e-mail, telephone number and a picture of her house to gp. He called her on the phone and they talked for over an hour and planned arrangements.

They made the arrangements to meet and true to his word, he booked a plane flight and found her house and met her. That was all that was needed. It was immediate love on both sides. So, annie then learned that love could span the miles no matter how long the distance. Today they are a committed couple and are extremely happy.

Tell me why
(written when mygrandniece was an infant)
By
Mary a. Laser

Tell me why there's springtime
Tell me why the rainbows shine
Tell me why the sky is blue,
And I will tell you just why I love you.
Because god made the springtime
Because god made the rainbows
Shine
Because god made the birds sing,
Too
Because god made you,
That's why I love you.
Tell me why there's summertime
Tell me why the sun does shine
Tell me why the flowers grow too,
And I will tell you just why I love you.
Because god made the summertime
Because god made the sun to shine
Because god made the flowers grow,
Because god made you
That's why I love you

Tell me why there's autumn time
Tell me why the stars do shine
Tell me why the leaves turn color
Too
And I will tell you just why I
Love you.
Because god made the autumn time

Because god made the stars to
Shine
Because god made leaves turn
Colors, too
Because god made you,
That's why I love you.
Tell me why there's wintertime
Tell me why the snow does shine
Tell me why there are snowflakes
Too, and I will tell you just why
I love you.
Because god made the wintertime
Because god made the snow to shine
Because god made the snowflakes
Too
Because god made you that's why I love
You.

A place to come home

Fiction
By
Mary a. Laser

They all lived together in a large home. Julia, shell, Maria, and a boarder named Sam. Julia had discussed for some time the fact that she would like to sell the house and move to a smaller apartment. Shell decided that she would go to Baltimore and live with a friend. Since they had little money, Maria asked Sam if he would like to share an apartment with her. After an at length conversation, they agreed that it would be in their mutual interest to do so. Sam was a handsome young man with a slight beard, gray eyes and dark hair. Maria was a slender girl with brown eyes and hair, and a lovely smile.

Sam and Maria agreed that they would find the apartment together, be responsible for half of all expenses, including food, and would put a certain percentage of what little money they made into a savings account. Both Sam and Maria were in college and worked almost full time. They further agreed that when they came home, they both would do the cooking and cleaning. In this way it would not present a burden on one person. A week later, they found an apartment that they could afford. It had only one bedroom, but since it had several large windows it could be fixed to place two beds with a divider.

Thanks to Julia, they were given two beds and other pieces of furniture. It turned out to be sufficient to furnish the apartment without frills. One of their neighbors had a truck and helped them move. Then the work began. The apartment needed some fixing up and they expended the effort to do it quickly.

Three weeks later, working evenings and what time they had on the weekends, the

Apartment was finished. They were extremely thankful that the woman who lived there had carpeting installed and it was just like new. Julia and shell came to see the apartment and were quite surprised to find it a lovely comfortable place.

As they walked through the door, all the closets and shelves were on the left side. The shelves were filled with items they needed to reach quickly, and clothes were in the closets. Next, at the end of the room was a very large window. There they placed two cozy chairs with a plant in-between and end tables on each side of the chairs. Continuing along the right side was the kitchen, small, but sufficient room for two people to work at the same time. Next was the door to the bedroom. They placed a light-colored blue curtain to separate the bedroom into two. It looked pleasant and neat, and each side had a window and a small closet. They found second hand end tables for each bed which were sufficient for them. For the next three years, they went to school, worked, and shared the cooking, cleaning, etc. As they had promised. Time went very quickly and after graduating they had sufficient funds saved to either rent a two-bedroom apartment or buy a small house. They opted for the house even though it meant having to start from scratch again. They continued with their education toward a masters' degree, while fixing up the house and working. Finally, at the end of a year, they had the house in great shape and it was truly lovely. There were two bedrooms and two baths and that was a special treat for them.

Three years later, maria decided to work full time and not return to college. Sam wanted to continue his education and go to medical school. After talking about what to do with the house, sam said if maria agreed He would like to keep it and he would use his savings to pay his share of expenses.

Graduation time came, and Maria was really proud of Sam -- he graduated cum laude. He was immediately given a position with the hospital and, in time with both of them working, they were able to pay off all of the bills and the house. Then the day came that Sam was offered a position that he could not afford to turn down. It was in another state, and although he was hesitating to go, he knew that he had to take the job. After a discussion, Sam asked Maria if she would keep the house and he would send money for his share of the expenses. That way, he said, he would always have a place to come home to.

Indeed, he did come home, holidays and weekends when he could get the time off. Gradually, however, he was unable to come home at all, but he kept his word and sent money to maintain the house. Two years went by and Maria found herself missing Sam more and more. She had to convince herself that he had his own life to live and she could not interfere. At the end of the third year, he called and said he would be coming home for Christmas. She was walking around on cloud nine and could not wait for that day to come. She knew then that she loved Sam very much, but obviously he did not feel the same way.

The doorbell rang Christmas Eve and when she answered it, she was shocked! Sam was even more handsome than ever and had a young lady with him. He introduced her as Sharon and said that he had been seeing her for a while and it could lead to marriage. When Sam told Sharon about our agreement with the house, she immediately said that Sam should sell it and take his share out of it. It would be a great down payment on a nice big house for her and Sam. Sam never answered her. Maria did not want to lose Sam completely, so that night she told him she would do whatever he wanted to do with the house. He said he would think about it.

As Sam and Sharon were leaving, he kissed Maria on the cheek and said that he would call her. She could hear Sharon telling him that

He should not be calling her, especially since they were living together.

The New Year began, and months went by without a call from Sam. Then, on Christmas Eve, the doorbell rang.

When Maria answered it, there was Sam. With a grin on his face, he told her he decided to come home for Christmas. She burst into tears and told him how happy she was to see him again. He took her in his arms and said that she was the only one he loved.

They were married on New Year's Day and it was the happiest day of their lives. Maria moved to be with Sam, but they kept the little house so they would always have a place to come home to.

The empty nest

Fiction
By
Katie (age 3) and Aunt Mary

Outside the big red brick home stands a tall pine tree. One day when Mrs. Robin was busy looking for the right tree to build her nest, she spotted the tall pine tree. This place, thought Mrs. Robin, is an ideal place to make a home. It is high enough and has many branches filled with pine needles-just the thing we need to keep the cats away. So, Mrs. Robin flew away to tell Mr. Robin of the nice spot she had selected. The next morning bright and early, Mr. Robin arrived and began collecting grass, twigs and even old string to build their nest. All through the day he labored and when evening came, he flew away. On the second day, both Mr. and Mrs. Robin returned and worked all day trying to complete the nest. Just before evening,

They were finished with their new home and moved right into the completed nest. The happy sounds that were heard meant they were very happy in their new home.

For many days, Mrs. Robin sat on her eggs in the nest while Mr. Robin brought food home for her to eat. Finally, the big day arrived and the eggs hatched. The robin family now had three baby robins in their family. Mother and father were kept very busy bringing food home to feed the little robins and each day the babies grew a little bigger and healthier. The days passed. During the sunny days, the babies were cool in the nest because the thick branches kept out the hot sun. During the windy days, they were safe because the parents had built a good strong nest. During the rainy days, they were snug and dry because part of the tall tree was located under the roof of the big red house and the rain could not get into the nest. One sunny Saturday morning in May, mother and father robin began chirping and flying around. They were starting to teach the babies to fly. One at a time the babies were coached out of the nest and taught how to use their wings. All day the baby robins were taught by their parents showing them how to flap their wings. Finally, evening came and all three babies were flying around having a wonderful time. "What a terrific feeling to be able to fly!" Said the baby robins. Soon, the parents told their children that it was time to go out on their own and find someone to love and make their own home. After many sad goodbyes, the baby robins flew into the sunset to find new homes for themselves. Mr. And Mrs. Robin stayed until the cold weather came, then they flew south to the warmer weather. Will the robins return? Only time will tell!

Cooking for a charity case

Fiction
By
Katie (my grandniece)

"He feels so hot" Casey said kindheartedly, looking at her little brother as she took her hand off his forehead. "I know. Unfortunately, I'm afraid he's going to have to stay here for a few more days, maybe even weeks", said the doctor. Casey's little brother Tyler had been ill for days now with a raging temperature that wouldn't seem to go down. Casey felt terrible for her brother because they were so close, and he was only six. Casey just sat with Tyler at the end of his hospital bed as he slept. "Casey, I'll be right back. Doctor, could I see you in the hallway for a second?" Asked Casey's mom. "Of course", replied the doctor. As Casey's mom and the doctor walked out of their room, Casey kept looking at her bother, "why does this have to happen to you?" she thought. Casey's mom started, "Doctor I really care for my son. I'd do anything in the world for him, but I do have to ask..." she started to whisper, "how much will this be costing me?" The doctor seemed a bit hesitant as he thought about the price. "You know Christine, I know that you care so much for your son, and I care for all of my patients, but I'm sorry to say, if we keep your son here much longer, which we will have to do, the price will be.....". The doctor wrote down the price on his clipboard and showed it to Christine. "Oh my" she remarked with a stunned look on her face. "i, I simply cannot afford it right now. Not now, or anytime soon! Please could we work something out?" "Please Ms. Carter, we cannot take your son out of our care. He is terribly ill and taking him out of this hospital would be a huge mistake. Ms. Carter, the results of that could be fatal!" Casey's mother was flabbergasted. She cared for her son more than anything in the world, but how could she ever afford something at that price? With only her part-time job and no one else to support her, there was just no possible way. When Casey's mother and doctor walked back into the room, Casey could see the disappointed look on her mother's face.

"Mom. What's wrong?" Casey asked

Sincerely. "Casey, nothing…nothing is wrong," her mom said plainly. Casey knew exactly what was wrong. Already that day she had heard her mother stressed over what the hospital bill might be like. "Casey," her mom said, "I think you should go home now. I'll stay with Tyler." Casey was a little upset. She didn't want to leave Tyler, but she saw how stressed her mother was. "Alright…see you at home," Casey told her mom. Then she walked out the hospital door. As Casey walked down the street back to her house, she was thinking of ways to earn more money for her mom and Tyler. She couldn't think of anything. She was too young for a job. Casey knew she had to find a way to save her brother. As she turned the corner she saw a bright green sign, 'bake off! Win!' there was other writing, but Casey couldn't read it. She didn't have to. The only word she

Needed to see was win. Casey went in closer to the sign:

Bake Off! WIN!
No prior experience needed.
Win $5,000 dollars!

Casey felt overjoyed. She'd found her way to earn the money! She quickly wrote her name down on the sign-up sheet and copied down the phone numbers and address. Then she ran home. Casey practiced baking lots of different things. She didn't know what she was going to have to bake for the contest. Although Casey was very new to baking, she caught on very quickly. Casey learned all of the tastes, smells, and textures of many different foods. She kneaded warm, floured dough under her hands, and felt cut-up, damp, fresh celery in the palms of her hands. She loved the sweet smells of fresh, out-of-the-oven chocolate cupcakes, and the taste of her homemade, creamy vanilla icing. Casey worked hard. Not only on learning how to prepare a chicken and learning how to make a fruit tart, but she also tried to memorize all the names and uses for the many different cooking utensils. "The cake comb is the one…that looks like a triangle…?" She'd have to remind herself. While her mother was in the hospital with Tyler, Casey really worked hard at getting everything right. She devoted most of her free time to baking until the competition. Right after school, she'd come home and get right on baking something. Anything. She'd usually call up her grandma and ask her for recipes, because her grandma was 'the queen' of cooking! Although Casey was having the time of her life playing with these new foods, this couldn't be all fun and games for her. She only had one and a half weeks left before the bake-off! She had to work fast at memorizing and preparing.

The next week went by fast. Casey had accomplished making 14 entrees in the last 11 days. She was awfully proud of herself because she had only started learning how to cook two weeks ago! She thought she was good, but there was always that doubt in the back of her mind that she wasn't good enough. She was sure that the other people at the bake-off would have much more experience in cooking than she did. But she had no more time to worry. The tournament was tomorrow, and she had to prepare herself. By the time she went to bed, she had practiced icing some cupcakes she had made the day before, she had finished up making some vegetable soup, and completed making a batch of lemon squares. It was the day of the tournament. Lucky for Casey she didn't have to let her mom know she was going because her mom was with Tyler at the hospital. Casey felt butterflies in her stomach as she walked down the street to the doors of the auditorium. She felt shaky, with nervous thoughts running through her head. "What if I forget how to turn the oven on? What if I'm not good enough? What if all of the people there are better than me?" Thinking these thoughts just made Casey feel sick. She needed to get ready! She walked through the doors of the gym. It had been transformed from the old, multi-use court to one big kitchen. There was a large crowd. There were ten cooking stations each set up with an oven, stove, refrigerator and sink. Casey was amazed at how many people there were! Although there were only ten contestants, there had to be 1,000 people there. Casey checked in with a lady at the front who was sitting at a long, brown table. Casey gave the woman her name, and the woman gave Casey a nametag and her number for which kitchen station to use. She walked over to her station. It was nothing like her own kitchen! But, she loved it. It was so nice and looked pretty expensive! "Contestants, please go to your stations," an announcer said. The noises that echoed throughout the gym slowly got quieter. "Hello, and welcome everyone to our 13th annual bake off!" Everyone clapped and there were a few cheers. "Now contestants, there will be three rounds. The first, making a pastry of your choice. Second, choosing the type of soup to make off a list we will provide. And last, preparing anything you'd like," said the announcer. Casey looked in her refrigerator and got out the ingredients to make some raspberry tarts. "Oh, and one more thing…" said the announcer slyly, "at the end of each round you will present your dish to the judges, and four people will be voted out each round." Casey's heart stopped. "Four people! A lot of these people are so much better than me!" Casey thought. She got so nervous. She had to do her absolute best. She decided not to make the tarts, instead she chose to make her creamy fudge filled chocolate cupcakes. Casey knew she was good at making them. "Ready?" Asked the announcer. "Set!" The whole auditorium got quiet. "Bake!" Casey felt her heart racing. She got all her ingredients together and started baking, and she was fast!

It only took 15 minutes for her to put together all ingredients and make the batter and the fudge. She baked the cupcakes, filled them with the fudge, and topped them with a sprinkle of powdered sugar. "Time's up!" Said the announcer. Everyone brought their foods up to the judges. About ten minutes later the announcer spoke again.

"Contestants, please step forward when you hear your number." Casey couldn't bear to listen. She closed her eyes, not focusing on anything. "9" said the announcer. "2, 6, 3,7, and 5." They all stepped forward: numbers 9, 2, 6,3,7. "um---number 5?" That was Casey's number. She still had her eyes closed tight. "Hey kid," said a tall man next to her, "I think that's you." Casey quickly went forward with hopefulness in her eyes. "Congratulations, you've made it to the next round!" Said the announcer. Casey was ecstatic! She had made it to the next round! She couldn't believe it! "Now, for this next round," the announcer said, "you have been given a list of soups you can choose from to make." Everyone rushed back to their stations. Casey looked over the list and decided to make a tomato soup. It was simple, plus she knew a secret ingredient to put into it, which she learned from her grandma. Once again Casey got out her ingredients and read over the recipe in her head. "Ready? Set? Bake!" Said the announcer. Casey once again put together a delicious soup and did it all

In an amazing amount of time! As it boiled in the pot, Casey smelled the delicious scent of the warm, creamy tomato soup. When it was finished, she poured it in a bowl and sprinkled a smidgen of parmesan cheese on top. "Time's brought their dishes over to the judges. This time, it was about 25 minutes before they got any results. Waiting longer made Casey feel even more anxious. Contestants, please step forward if you hear your number called, said one of the judges. 9, 6,3, and 7. Said the judge. Casey's number had not been called. She felt disappointed and oozing with nervousness at the same time. She knew that her cooking wasn't going to be good enough! It was time for her to just go home… "I'm sorry, but you have been eliminated. "Congratulations contestants numbers 2 and 5!" Said the judge. Casey

was in shock. She timidly took a step forward, as her whole body felt
shaky and she couldn't quite see straight. "Had they really called my
number?" She thought. As Casey looked around nearly in a daze, she
met the eyes of the other contestant next to her who had also made it
to the final round. She was smirking at Casey. "Pathetic. I'm left with
a child? Well, good luck, let's not make mommy disappointed." Said
the woman with an attitude. Casey said nothing, but just smiled at the
woman. Inside she felt furious. Casey snapped out of her dreams and
put on her game face. She knew that she had made it this far and she
needed to win the money for her mom and Tyler. "Alright contestants,
back to your stations. For the last round you can make anything of
your choice. Have fun with it!" Said the announcer. Casey walked back
to her station. She had decided to make another type of cake-a black
bottom cake. It is a chocolate layered cake that is topped with cream
cheese flavored icing with a chocolate chip layer---- a specialty from her
grandmother. Again, she got out her ingredients and went to the recipe
in her head. "Ready contestants? Get set, bake!" Said the announcer.
Casey rushed to get everything together and start baking. Gathering
the shortening, frosting, sugar, vanilla, chocolate chips, eggs, flour
and anything else she could get her hands on. She worked flawlessly;
mixing the cake batter, whipping the frosting, baking and frosting the
cake perfectly. Casey got the cake to come out beautifully. She was so
thrilled with it! She'd never baked anything as intricate as this cake.
"Contestants, time's up! Please bring your dishes to the judge's table,"
said the announcer. "Hmm, I'd like to see what that nasty old lady
has made," thought Casey with a smirk. As Casey walked up to the
judge's table with all her pride in her hands, she looked over at the other
woman's dish. It looked beautiful and delicious. It was a small roast
fully prepared with celery, onions and carrots. Casey knew she wanted
some of that dish. It looked absolutely irresistible. Casey looked at her
small cake and felt that it could not compare to the woman's meal.
Casey felt defeated already. She was definitely not going to win now.
She still brought her cake up to the judge's table with a worried look

on her face. The other woman brought up her dish, and Casey could see the delighted look on the judge's faces. Great! Thought Casey sarcastically.

Casey and the other woman stood side-by-side for at least 15 minutes. Faintly Casey heard some noise from the judge's area. She looked over and saw three, then four of the judges coughing with a disgusted look on their faces. Casey wondered what this meant. "Did they just judge my cake? Oh no!" She thought to herself. Another 15 minutes went by, and the judges had finally finished. "Hello contestants," said one of the judges politely. Casey knew the game was over for her right now. "Well, we've tasted both your dishes, and I'd personally like to announce the winner of the $5,000!" There was clapping from the audience. "Well…" started the judge, "after tasting both dishes…" Casey could not wait until they announced the other woman's name. She felt absolutely sick to her stomach. "I'd like to proudly

Announce…" "Here it goes!" Thought Casey. "the winner is…" Casey was shaking, "Contestant number 5, Casey carter!"

There was clapping and cheering from the audience, and one big gasp from the woman next to her. Casey was stunned. How could she have won? She stood absolutely still, then shakily walked up to the judges and thanked them with all her heart, then gladly accepted the check for $5,000. "What!!" Screamed the other woman? "How could I have not won?!" "Well ma'am," said one of the judges calmly, "your dish certainly did look beautiful, but the meat inside was not cooked thoroughly. It was quite raw actually."

The woman was absolutely astonished and fiercely angry. She stomped away. Casey felt like the most amazing person in the world, holding that check in her hands. She ran right to the hospital. When she arrived at her brother's room, she saw Tyler in his hospital bed, with her mom holding his hand. "Mom!" Casey exclaimed. "Yes, hello Casey," her mom said with a laugh, "what's the matter?" "Mom, I have a surprise for you. I know that things have been hard for you

with the bills from the hospital, and having to keep Tyler here, but…
Casey pulled out the $5,000- check. "Here," said Casey. Her mother
took it from Casey and held it in her hands. She looked amazed and
taken aback. "Casey! Where did you get this money?" Questioned her
mother. "I entered a contest and I won! Well, I had to work for it, but,
I got the money! And, I did it for Tyler and you!" Said Casey proudly.
"Casey…" said her mother still stunned, "shouldn't we put this away
for you? For college, or something…" said her mother. "No, you and
tyler need it much more now than I will later," Casey said smiling at
her mom. "Casey, you are---are-- definitely the best daughter a mother
could have," said her mother nearly in tears. Casey and her mother
embraced, and her mother felt the world lifted off her shoulders. So,
for the rest of the day, they all just sat there and talked. Casey knew
that she had definitely done something worthwhile.

The long road to destiny

Fiction
By
Joey vendetto jr. (my grandnephew)

Nilea, a harsh and dead land. Only fools dare to enter. There is no normal life, no living plants, no hope, and no dreams. Dead trees, bushes, and underbrush are scattered across this dying land, … in the center of nilea lies mt. Hiera. Mt. Hiera is nearly as tall as everest. However, the climate is not the same. It never snows or rains. The mountain itself is a tall dark peak stretching into the black sky. The only color on the mountain is white from the bones and skulls of xar's meal. Xar is a dragon; a magical being thought to be dead for 1,000 years but still lives. Xar's minions, sala-men, are snake/lizard hybrids. They are snake from the waist down and salamander waist up. These hybrids come in many different forms and colors. Some have venomous bites, while some don't. Some have the strength to lift a sword or spear, while others fight with their claws. But one thing you want to always avoid is seeing one turn bright red. Red means they have become furious and will stop at nothing to kill you, not even suicide. Their leader, silvaian, allied with xar after the great forty second war. The forty second was the whole race of sala-men battling humans, elves, gnomes, and dwarfs. The entire gnome race was destroyed; however, the sala-men were no match for the rest of them. Led by scaven who forced the sala-men into nilea, was knighted and afterwards by king gheed himself. The sala-men who had a few men left (about 100), allied with xar in hope of protection. Afterward, xar's reign of terror began. He began destroying villages killing men, women and children without any challenge. Soon he was able to control minor creatures and use them for his army and for his meals. Soon he destroyed one-fourth of the world's population of humans, dwarfs, and elves alike. Now something was about to happen that xar never had in mind.

A druid, paladin, mage, and archer will team up and try to destroy xar. In fairy tales the good guys would win an easy victory and the world would celebrate and rejoice. However, is this an average fairy tale?

Chapter one: Long days ahead

King gheed sat on his throne looking at his beloved city of bultain when unexpected news arrived. "my lord..." came a high-pitched nervous voice. What is it, gheed demanded studying his servant. Terrible news, terrible news! The town of zul'daran, just three miles north of here, has been destroyed! There were no survivors, but we expect it to be the work of xar." "xar...," gheed murmured. "blast him! We have no choice but to evacuate the city! We're bound to be his next target!" "indeed, but I think I have an idea!" The servant cried happily. "maybe if we...no, all of us team up to kill this monster!" Gheed shook his head sadly. "no, I cannot risk putting my kingdom in danger." "maybe we can send our finest warriors like...that sir scaven?!" "yes..." pondered gheed. "he is a

Superb warrior and he knows a little white magic." "oh! And what about jakque the druid? Or umm, gar! He's a mage! You know the saying 'fight fire with fire? Fight magic with magic?'" jakque was a druid who lived in the wiles forest. Druids focused on the power of nature and animals. He had a unique ability to change into a werewolf whenever there was a full moon, and it did not have to be full. While gar was an expert mage, he did not have a lot of common sense, but he was one of the best mages in the world. He focused mainly on fire and ice-type spells. He enjoyed ice because as he said, "ice is my favorite because it does not leave a mess after using it." He would just create an ice ball, freeze his enemy, and then just kick it—shattering his enemy to tiny bits. "well, I guess we have to." Gheed said sadly. "send word across the land of the noble heroes! I want them to eat free at every tavern and sleep soundly at every inn." "when shall I send word?" The servant asked. Gheed smiled, "now."

Chapter two: the beginning

Sir scaven was making a pot of herbal tea when he heard a knock on the door. He sighed, smoothed his ash black hair, and got up. It's been so long since he did anything. No one he knew could beat him in a sword battle, and training was beginning to become monotonous and easy. "I really must do something." He thought looking at his paling hands. He opened his door, looked out, and saw a royal guard holding a parchment to him. He spoke with a delicate and fancy english accent. "by order of king gheed you are to set out on a quest to kill the dragon xar." The guard paused to let it sink in. "this should explain everything." The guard shoved the parchment to him. "you will have two other allies. Possibly three. Jacque and gar will be your allies and we have word of another joining your party. Well, good day sir." With that he walked up the road and soon out of sight. Scaven sat on his chair thinking wildly. "what? Kill xar? Him?! He killed thousands of men and women without

Caring! Then again…i have no choice…" a voice in his head began ringing. "choice? Ha! Just

A few seconds ago you said you want action! You want to do something! Now you deny it? What a pity. I guess years made you more frightened of your own shadow."

Scaven shook his head. He opened the scroll and read the whole thing until something caught his eye: along the way to mount hiera, the elf dak tan will join your party.

He read it at least thrice. An elf? Scaven hadn't had an elven ally for about five years. He hasn't seen one since the forty second war. He sighed and walked over to a large chest. It was an old brown cedar chest. It's been five years since he last opened it. He gripped the lid and swung it open cautiously like something would jump out and attack. He looked in there and saw his plate mail and sword. Actually, the sword was his father's. His armor consisted of a skullcap like helmet, Reddish-brown gauntlets, greaves, and his plate mail. He looked at the golden cross in

The center of the plate mail, which was only visible if it caught light. Then, he reached out and touched his father's sword. He

Gently picked it up inspecting it on how much it changed in the last five years. It had gold

Embedded into the handle and small pieces of topaz scattered around in the side of it. He chuckled; his father always liked fancy jewelry. His father used it proudly in every battle. But scaven only used it in special battles. Like the forty second war. He closed his eyes as a dark memory came upon him, an evil memory. 30 years ago, when he was very young (about age 5), he remembered his mother running in sobbing wildly. After scaven asked what happened, his mother looked at him darkly. His father was killed in battle. But not just any battle, a battle with the sala-men. How was he able to remember this at such a young age? He gritted his teeth, he knew that memory would be burned into his mind forever. He pulled out the parchment again. It said to meet in town at 8:00 a.m. Sharp. He smiled and said, "I have a lot of packing to do."

Chapter three: the first step

Sir scaven stood there in the middle of the crowd. His father's sword in his hilt, and his armor tied up nice and tight in his backpack. All around him people were talking amongst

Themselves. "ooohh mommy. Is he going to get rid of that mean dragon?"

"can he bring a scale home?" "yea a scale! Wouldn't that be so neat?" "I wish I were like him." The children were mainly talking, calling and yelling to each other. Then he heard a familiar voice yelling and talking and growing nearer to him. "yes, yes, it's a lovely bird…no, it is not a chicken! How am I s'posed to know what it tastes like? It's a dove…. Yes, it's a dove! No, it is not a bloody chicken! Geez…" sir scaven knew who that was: jakque. She was a druid who lived in the local forest. She had a beautiful dove that was even whiter than snow, as she said. She was pretty nice too, but if you insult her or make her angry, you'll wish you never met her! She had shoulder length brown hair, and she wore leather/wool baggy robes. She

Held a staff that looked almost like a cross between a snake and a dead tree. And on her

Other shoulder, sat her majestic dove: blizzard.she ran up and greeted him warmly."scaven how long has it been? Five years? Oh right, you're a 'sir' now,

Sir scaven smiled back. "you can still call me scaven. What was up with that chicken thing?" She frowned. "oh, a bunch of 4-year-olds thinking blizzard was a chicken."

Jakque gently tapped blizzard's head. Just then out of the crowd gar appeared. "scaven! Jakque!" Cried gar happily. "it has been at least five years since i've seen you-wow jakque, what's with the chicken on your shoulder?!" Jakque's face went bright red, and her voice went from a cheerful call to a booming scream. "blizzard is not a chicken why do you people…" Gar held up a hand for silence. "jakque, five years and you still can't take a simple joke." Gar wore a blue robe with silver buttons; he had leather boots and light gloves. He had red long hair that made him look like it had not been cut for at least two years and seemed to be a

Little pale. "attention! All hail king gheed! Everyone looked up and saw king gheed and a

Finely dressed guard. Everyone bowed toward gheed and gheed began to speak proudly. "as you all know the demon xar plagued our lands and is doing his best to destroy all of us! However, these three heroes bravely volunteered to smite this demon!" He literally drafted us sir

Scaven thought. Then that annoying voice in his head began to speak: "nay, you want to avenge your father's death….of course I want to, but gheed, he's being a pig!" You are still angry. It's difficult for you to accept the fact you will never ever see him again. So obviously you're angry because your father was drafted. Yes, dead dead. Gone. Gone…never to see you again! "scaven!" Gar shouted worriedly looking at him. "are you all right? You were mumbling, and it seemed like you weren't with us!" "oh, i-i'm fine. Perfectly fine! Just a little dizzy." Scaven muttered trying to cover up what happened. "if you say so." Gar turned back to gheed. "and now we supply you with maps and your

Passes to inns and taverns. Now, if you please, givajin." The guard, givajin, then

Handed each of them a map. All of them shoved it into their pockets and backpacks. "and now heroes, I bid you farewell." Gheed smiled and walked off.

Chapter four: the long road

The three of them stood there, looking up the road."well, which way do we go?" Asked gar. Scaven began, "they say the quickest way from two points is a straight line. However, that won't apply here. The safest way is to travel six miles on feolony road, arrive at leobnze, go through the zel'gan forest, travel up dead man's road and arrive at nilea. Hmm, it appears there's a 1/5-mile-long bridge!" Gar whistled. "that's one long bridge. How do you s'pose they made it?"

"mages or dwarves' you imbecile!" Jakque snapped. "okay then," gar began, where this fenze, fenzo, ferry, furry…uhhh…is" "for the love of-it's feolony road and it's right behind you!" Jakque clutched her throat.

"I swear you're going to give me a stroke!" Gar turned around to see an aged sign in white letters pointing up a trail marked:

Feolony Road

"Everyone shush!" Scaven ordered.

"What?" "shush!" They stood there for a minute. Gar flinching and wincing. Jakque stood as still as a statue while blizzard gave out little chirps and sounds of interest. But scaven stood listening at a patch of grass. Then a sound. A sound of movement. All at once, an orange lizard the size of scaven's index finger ran out. Giving out...a cry? Scaven grabbed it, pushing his thumb and index finger on its neck to prevent it from biting him. "Who are you? I know you can speak. So, speak!" Scaven yelled menacingly. The lizard began to gasp for breath, and then in a high-pitched voice...it spoke! "Oh, umm, I am papair! Yes, I am! And I was eh...looking for strawberries! They are yummy, yes? Very juicy! You be seeing any strawberries?" Scaven raised his sword to papair's head. "I did not want to work for xar, no I didn't! He would have killed me! I had no choice!"

Gar seized papair from scaven examining him. But gar made a mistake! He was holding papair by the tail! Papair flipped up and bit gar's hand! "gah, the little bugger!" Gar clutched his arm trying to stop the pain. Scaven tried to hold gar down, but he kept kicking and yelling. "Get it!" Jakque pointed to papair who was scurrying into the bushes and deeper into the forest. Jakque made a grab for him but missed and fell.

"Stupid human!" Papair cried. "Humans are too bulky! They're too fat, too slow!" "screeeeeech!" Blizzard was on papair's tail! His wings flapping madly, talons ready to make a grab for him! The brilliant white dove was getting closer and closer papair thought. "the river! Yes, I will be safe there! I can lose the bloody bird there!"

Blizzard made a grab for papair and missed! But in seconds, the unique bird was on papair's tail once again! Papair saw it up ahead… the river! Papair jumped in, sticking

His forked tongue at blizzard. With all his might, he tried to pounce on papair, but it

Was too close to a series of rocks! Blizzard hit the rocks, stumbled on them, and then fell head first into the water. He tried to fly out, but he couldn't! He was too weak, too tired. Minutes later blizzard washed up onto the shore and laid there trying to restore his fatigue. He stood up, bowed his head so freezing water dripped off his beak, and flew off sadly to jakque. "Oh my gosh," scaven whispered to jakque, "It's poisonous! We have to get him to a priest! We have to get to leobnze!" "But it's at least four hours away!" "We have to try! Or gar is a goner!" Jakque looked at gar's hand. "Look!! It's already spreading! Scaven, don't you know any form of magic to save him?" Scaven let his head dri can't risk it, we don't even know what kind of poison this is!" Just then jakque felt a cold breeze, then something damp dropped onto her shoulder. There, perched on her shoulder, was blizzard. He was sneezing and giving out little cries of his sad song. "Oh, you poor thing!" Jakque held Blizzard who was still soaking wet. "jakque, i'm sure blizzard will be fine, but for now we really need to help gar!" Scaven grabbed gar's arms and placed them on his shoulders. After jakque placed blizzard into her backpack to keep him warm, she then took gar's legs and put one underneath each arm. Making sure he was secure, they ran off to leobnze as fast as they could. Along the way jakque asked scaven, "how can a mere lizard do this?" Scaven didn't answer for about 10 minutes until he said, "I don't think that was a lizard.

Chapter five:

xar papair stood there on a rock laughing, bird thinks he can fool me! Ha! So silly it be! Now, where is my ride? Eh?" Then out of a tree popped an odd creature. A hippogriff! Hippogriffs were once peace-loving animals until xar corrupted them with his evil magic.

From hips up they were an eagle, but they had long yellow horns, almost like a deer. And from the hips down, was a body of a lion."to xar, you tree hugger. Heh, I like that, tree hugger." Papair, with some difficulty, climbed onto it and grabbed onto its neck. The hippogriff took off with a Gallop, then floated into the air, going a rough 50 miles an hour. About an hour later they arrived at the summit of mt. Hiera. He peered into the dark cave where xar was. "Now tree hugger, stay here and we may let you have some fresh food for once." Papair began stumbling in. "gah, we really should get a better method of transportation!" Then a low voice shouted, "Well, what do you expect? A nice, safe, flying horse and buggy ride?" Xar looked at papair, his long black talons scratching on the stone floor. He smiled at papair, revealing at least 100 razor sharp teeth. His eyes glowed an evil blue, while he had short pointy ears and a long slithering tail. And, scariest of all, he had blackish-blue scales. Xar's den was at the summit of mt. Hiera. There was very little there. To the left was a pile of skeletons from his meals. To his right was a huge hole where xar entered and exited as he pleased. Which was also the way papair came. So, Papair, any news? Papair walked up and bowed. "Master, three humans are coming to kill you! But there is luck!

They are very Puny and weak! I bit one! And you know my poison, it can kill quickly. A papair, describe these humans to me!" Xar ordered. "Oh yes, yes. One was a druid with a pain-in-the-neck dove...another was a warrior and a mage! I poisoned the mage! He should not last long."

"When will they arrive?" "ummm, anywhere from tomorrow to next week." He smiled. "If they get past the forest. Oh yes, the forest. Now, if you please, I need to be alone to think. Of course, master, of course! Papair ran over to the hippogriff, jumped onto it and yelled, "to the hippogriff farm!" Papair sped off, yelling at the poor creature.

"Now," xar began to think aloud, "I wonder if they would take the long way up here? Hmm. Perhaps I better go tell silvaian to clear the mountain of most of his men. I want to fight them alive, untouched, and fresh!" Xar licked his lips. "I don't know why, but the ones with muscle always tasted better." Xar

Yawned, then curled up into a ball dreaming of his pushover opponents.

Chapter six: leobnze

It was night when they arrived at leobnze. Scaven's and jakque's limbs felt like they would collapse or even fall off any moment.

"Look!" Panted scaven. He was pointing to a large stone building. It had stain glass windows of mainly christian heroes. And on top was a large cross, which was surrounded by candles lighting it up like a single leaf on a bare tree. Scaven and jakque burst through the doors sweating and panting, yet still holding gar. The priest looked up without an expression. He looked like a short human or a tall dwarf. He wore a long white cloak, which covered his whole body except for his nose and mouth. He motioned for them to lay gar onto the floor. After they carefully placed him onto the floor, the priest examined him carefully. The infection was in his whole arm and was working its way into the rest of his body.

"joachim, virgil, tyranal! Get the opinol medicine too! Hurry, we don't have much time!" He spoke with a deep voice. He was definitely a dwarf. Then, scaven remembered: "opinol medicine? That was for snakebites. Or rattlesnake bites! If this was a serious as a rattlesnake, then…. Gar may not make it.the dwarven priest, followed by three humans carried gar into a back room behind the pews. "wait! Is he going to make it?" Scaven called out. The priest turned around and sighed. We'll give him the medicine and perform the surgery, but there's still a chance he won't—we will do all we can." The priest bowed and walked into the back room and closed the door behind him. Jakque sighed sadly, then shouted, "Blizzard!" She looked into her backpack and saw blizzard and he was sleeping. He looks healthy," scaven said cheerfully, "now let's find an inn, i'm tired. We can check on gar tomorrow." As they walked out of the church, they saw a sign that said:

> **VELINDOR'S INN AND BAR**

The whole place looked cheerful and it didn't look too crowded either. As they walked in, they realized they didn't have any money. Wait, maybe showing them gheed's note would help. They walked into the inn and were merrily greeted by the innkeeper. Greetings strangers, welcome! I'm velindor, what can I do for you?" "oh yes," scaven began, "we wish to stay for a night and have a meal. We would like a room with two beds, it does not have to be too fancy either. We will be out before dawn. Oh, I have this!" Scaven pulled out his note and handed it to him. "oh, this is indeed his signature. Well, ok. What would you like for dinner?" "i'll have roasted chicken."

"And i'll have a salad." Jakque piped up.

"Of course. I'll tell the cook. Oh! And your room is #15." Velindor walked over to the cook, whispered their order and went back to his post at the front door. Jakque and scaven went to the counter and sat down. Then a middle-aged man walked up to them. He wore a brown robe and had gray hair. He handed the food to each one. you didn't use magic to make this, did you?" Scaven asked. "I'm sorry, but it seems everything is done by magic these days." "Oh, no!" He replied. "Everything is pre-made, but it tastes like its freshly picked or just out of the oven. Say, where are you heading anyway?"

"zul'gan forest." Scaven replied with a mouth full of food. "What's your name? I never caught it?" "Well, i'm sir scaven, or scaven, and this is jakque. Well now, scaven and jakque, they say zul'gan forest is haunted. Haunted? "Some travelers pass through safe without seeing a thing, while some never return. Of course, these are simply rumors, but still. They say there are skeletons too, and the only way to knock them out for good is to smash their skuls. Oh gee, that makes me feel good." Muttered jakque. "Look, it's only a rumor. I've never been there myself. Well, i'm busy, enjoy your dinner and have a goodnight!" "Yes… thank you." Scaven replied slowly.

Chapter seven: the dead stand ready

Jakque and scaven stood at the foot of the church. Blizzard stood on jakque's shoulder looking healthier than ever.

"Well, let's go…" scaven sighed and walked in. To his delight, there stood gar smiling at them. "He's made a full recovery." The priest smiled happily. But I warned him not to cast spells for at least 24 hours. You see, we had to go pretty deep into his hand and if he casts a spell, he would, umm, how do I put this? Well, his hand would explode. So, don't cast spells for one day. Now I must go. May the lord be with you. Gar walked over to them, pulling at the cloth wrapped around his hand. He asked, "So…to zul'gen forest?"

"To zul'gen forest." Scaven replied.

They crossed the long stone bridge and along the way scaven told gar about the skeletons. Gar in return, looked at them like they were crazy. Soon they arrived at the entrance. As they entered, they felt a chill run down their spines. It was dark; trees were so big they covered the sun. "Well, we're supposed to meet the elf somewhere around here," scaven said. When they were half-way through the forest, they heard a whoosh, and right next to scaven's head was a dagger! He looked around trying to figure out where it came from and there, to his horror, was a skeleton! It had bleach white bones and near its grinning skull, it held knives—only four, but it still made scaven feel uneasy. Then about 30 more appeared. Some had arrows, some had swords, and some had javelins all aimed at the three of them. "Oh my gosh…" gar said trembling. "Remember, try to smash their skulls! Gar, you need to stay here and try to remain safe." After scaven gave out the orders, jakque raised her staff to them, and scaven pulled out his father's sword. "Attack!" Scaven cried as he plunged for one of the 31 skeletons! Scaven cut off the skeleton's head, but before the skeleton could pick it up, scaven stepped on it causing the skull and skeleton to turn to ash. Scaven felt an arrow cut his cheek. It nearly went into his head. "scaven!" Called jakque. "Do you think I can transform into a werewolf here? Its day, but the trees make it seem like night." "Go ahead and give it a shot!" Scaven cried back. Jakque raised her staff in the sky and chanted, "Strength of the moon hear my call, of when these monsters and demons will fall! Strength of the west and strength of the east, show these creatures the beast!" Jakque's back began to twist forward. Her limbs, then her whole body was covered in a thick fur. She began to have an appearance of a large wolf. Soon her eyes glowed an eerie red and she grew fangs. Jakque was now a werewolf! She let out a blood-curdling scream and began smashing the skeletons like they were toothpicks. But, after about 15, she grew tired and since they were aiming for her, she was the most damaged.

Gar watched hopelessly as his friends were getting beaten! Scaven was getting worn out and bruised, while jakque was a bloody mess. It was a terrible sight, and there were still about 15 more skeletons left! Suddenly, a young voice cried out, "hey, watch it guys! If you're not careful, you're going to get killed!" Suddenly an elf hopped

Down from a tree and began firing arrows rapidly at the skeletons. He stood near gar and spoke quickly. "Hello, my name is dak'tan. I can see you're being ambushed by a bunch of cursed beings. Wait. You have the looks of a mage. Can't you help?" But in seconds the skeletons were all turned into ash. Soon, everyone ran out of the woods, up dead man's road and without stopping, dropped into the edge of nilea. Everyone lay there gasping for breath. Jakque changed back from a werewolf and lay on the ground staying very still. They all stared into the cloudy sky of nilea until dak'tan spoke. Greetings, as I said earlier, i'm dak'tan and i'm going to say you're my allies who are going to help kill xar? Everyone sat up and began talking and introducing themselves to dak'tan. Anyway, I could have taken them out easily with a cold spell," bragged gar. "Oh well, I think I can cast spells now. Good thing, too!"

"Yes, okay my friends, but we must go now! Time is of the essence!"

Chapter eight: silvaian's battle

The four of them ran quickly through nilea and up to mt. Hiera. "Look, what's that?" Gar asked, pointing to an acre big pen. It appeared to have hippogriffs in it, and they were chained to the fence! "Hmm, hippogriffs. Can we use them to ride to the top of the mountain? We can try but look what else is there! It's the sala'men leader! Silvaian! Dak'tan cried pointing to the cage. But ssilvaian spotted them and was heading right for them! He opened his hands and on each finger was a long talon. "if you want to battle xar, you must get by me. Without another word, silvaian leaped up onto gar, forcing him down and snapping at his throat. Scaven lifted his sword and swung it rapidly at silvaian, but the lizard dodged every move. "ziliko kelthos!" Gar shot a ball of ice at silvaian, but just as he dodged it scaven cut off half of its tail! Silvaian screamed and then turned a bright red. Jakque was whacking at it while blizzard was pecking at its head and beak (a lot of good that did). But it smacked blizzard away and grabbed jakque's staff and threw it at her. It hit her pretty hard, but just knocked her unconscious for about a minute. She fell onto dak'tan, which caused him to flip over, thusly scattering his arrows everywhere and knocked the bow out of his hand. Gar was about to cast a spell but silvaian bit his arm exactly where he had surgery done. He gasped in pain clutching his arm. This left only one person: sir scaven. The sala'men jumped on him, squeezing his arms making them feel like they would fall off. He tried to stop him, but he couldn't. He knew for sure silvaian would end his. "ziliko kelthos!" An ice ball hit silvaian in the back. The lizard stood there frozen solid. Everyone stood up at least half alive. "Okay, everyone alright?" Scaven announced. Gar walked up to the frozen sala'man. "What a pity. If only he was stone. Excellent yard ornament, don't you think?" He kicked the frozen lizard shattering it to pieces. "See jakque, I told you cold spells work the best!" "Can we just get on with this?" Jakque announced wobbling around, still not fully recovered from her unconsciousness.

Chapter nine: the final battle

After about an hour of resting they went over to the hippogriffs. Scaven cut four of them loose and everyone boarded their own. "watch, order your hippogriff to the summit of the mountain like the summit of mt. Hiera!"

Scaven's hippogriff began running in a circle until it rode up in the air and started floating straight up the mountain. Everyone else ordered the same thing. Gar held on tight to his. He looked down and almost fainted. He looked down about 2,000 feet and they were traveling upwards 100 feet every second. When they got to the top, gar had a hard time letting go. He jumped into the cave and walked around while his knees felt like a type of gelatin. They looked in, adjusting their eyes to the darkness, and then they saw him. In the middle of the room stood xar. Xar looked at them and laughed loudly. "Look," xar yelled, "let's make this quick, I got a town to destroy and i'm thinking about bultain. Oh, yes, isn't that your village? Hmm?" "zinca nelicop." Gar shot an electric web at xar, but he broke free instantly. Dak'tan shot arrows at his eyes.

"Good, keep it up, dak'tan!" Encouraged scaven. "I only have about six arrows left!" He cried back nervously. Jakque hummed a tune and out of the floor shot roots tangling xar and forcing him to the ground. He blew a breath of fire that burned them off of him. Then he put his head back and spat out what you might call ice breath, randomly around the room.

"Duck!" Scaven started hacking at xar's scales, but they were too thick and strong. Suddenly he had a plan! "jakque, distract xar and try to hold him down with your root spell! Dak'tan, shoot for xar's eyes! And gar, cast a spell on xar's stomach and see if you can destroy his scales!" Jakque ran around repeating the spell trapping xar, but xar repeated his escape. However, dak'tan was able to blind xar's left eye, but afterwards he didn't have any arrows left so he joined jakque in distracting him. Then, xar grabbed dak'tan and threw him against the wall, knocking him unconscious. Gar sent a huge ice blast at Xar's stomach. Then scaven hit him with his sword. The scales shattered!

Now xar's bare skin remained unprotected. With all his strength, he shoved his sword into xar's stomach. Blue sparks followed. Xar turned into blue fire, then disintegrated. Then, it felt like an earthquake started up.

"This whole place is collapsing! Quick, we got to get out of here!" Gar shouted as he jumped onto his hippogriff. Scaven jumped onto his and then he shouted, "dak'tan!" "I got him!" Answered jakque. She picked up his unconscious body and laid him onto her hippogriff. As she started to descend, a cold breeze hit dak'tan waking him up. He had no idea what happened, so he fell off. However, jakque grabbed him just in time. "I'm slipping!" Dak'tan shouted. "Hold on!" Jakque ordered. Dak'tan was pulling her off her hippogriff and she had to grab onto its antler to stay on. Then, for what seemed like a century, they arrived at the bottom. Everyone got off and stared at the mountain, watching it crumble. Then, out of the sky his father's sword flew and fell in front of him.

He picked it up, but it was now bent out of shape. The blade was too delicate, and the handle could be easily crushed. He sighed happily. There was no adventure more fantastic than this was.

Epilogue:

When the four heroes returned, they were all knighted (except for sir scaven, since he was already knighted). From that day on, sir scaven never had another adventure. He claims that all others would bore him after what he went through all sala'men were destroyed since they gave their life to xar and xar no longer exists, neither do they. But one small problem remains……. Papair! Who is actually a baby dragon! However, that will be another story.

The little rabbit who ran away

Fiction by
Katie (my grand niece)

Once upon a time, there was a family of rabbits who lived in a farmer's barn. The farmer was very good to the rabbits and when the last little boy rabbit was born, the farmer named him henry. Mom and dad rabbit liked the name and so they agreed that their baby boy would be called henry. Henry had a brother and a sister and although his siblings were very good and listened to mom all the time, henry decided he wanted to do whatever he felt like doing and would not listen.

One lovely sunny morning, mom rabbit told her children that she wanted them to take a nice nap after breakfast and then they would go visiting down the lane and in the woods. Henry said to himself, "I am not going to take a nap, I am going to run away and see Things for myself." So, as soon as everyone was asleep, henry slipped out of the barn and ran off down the road. The first thing he saw was a snake. "Oh snake," he said, "are you running away also?" "No, no." Said the snake, "I want to be with my family, I would not want to run away." So, off ran henry and a little later he saw a bear. "Oh bear," he asked, "are you running away?" "No, I am not," replied the bear, "I am going in the woods to play with my sister." So off went henry on his journey. Soon, he came to a rooster sitting on a log crowing cock-a-doodle-do. "Excuse me," called henry, "are you running away?"

"Me, run away?" Replied the rooster. "No, no I love to sit here and make my special sounds."

Now henry was getting a little bored going off all by himself, but he continued on down the road. When he looked up, he realized he was lost. Now he was scared, and he said to himself, "I must stay calm. I know, I will turn around and follow my foot steps back."

So, henry followed his footsteps and sure enough he saw the rooster, then he saw the bear and then he saw the snake. He began running as fast as he could to get to his home. When he reached home, his family was just waking up from their nap. "Oh mommy," henry cried. "I ran away from home and I will never do that again. I am so happy to be home with my family." Mother rabbit hugged henry and said she was happy to have him home again also. Then she asked if he wanted to go for a walk with the family and meet all of the neighbors. "no thank you mom," replied henry, "I just want to snuggle up and take a nap and wait for you all to come home."

Little raindrop's good deed

Fiction by
Katie and aunt mary

Once upon a time, there was a little raindrop who lived high up in the clouds. Every day the little raindrop looked over the cloud and down at the lovely big earth below.one day the raindrop saw a little girl planting a seed. She carefully dug up the earth, made a hole, put her seed in to the hole and covered it up with dirt. It so happened that the weather was very dry and, of course without rain, her seed could not grow. The little girl wanted it to rain so very much, but there was just no rain at all. The little raindrop felt very sorry for the girl as he watched her from his cloud. He wanted to come down to earth to help her, but the little raindrop's mother said he was too small to go down to help the little girl's seed grow all by himself. The little raindrop was so sad, he cried. Then, as he heard Mr. Thunder go by, he got a good idea. He quickly

Ran around the big cloud and soon he had many, many little raindrops gathered together. They asked their parents' permission to jump down to earth to help the little girl's seed grow. Their parents were so happy that the little raindrops wanted to do a good deed that they allowed the raindrops to go to earth. All at the same time, holding hands, the little raindrops jumped over the cloud and came gently falling down to earth—landing right on top of the planted seed. Soon the seed began to come up through the ground and started to bloom. When the little girl saw the bloom, she was so very happy, she did not know what to do! And to this very day, the little girl never knew that because a little raindrop wanted to do a good deed, her seed turned into a beautiful flower.

And that is the end.

Mary A. Laser

Born in Pennsylvania, author of 2 books. "The boy from Beirut" and "memoirs of a command sgt. Major" She was a member of the u.s. Military for three years. Upon discharge she was called back to walter reed army medical center where she was assigned as an administrator. She worked there for 33 ½ years. Upon retirement she became a realtor for ten years and then began writing. This is her third book titled "Prayers That God Will Hear".